CAVES

Conceived and created
by Claude Delafosse
and Gallimard Jeunesse
Illustrated by Héliadore

HIDDEN WORLD

A FIRST DISCOVERY BOOK

SCHOLASTIC INC.
New York   Toronto   London   Auckland   Sydney
Mexico City   New Delhi   Hong Kong

Incredible scenery
and large open
spaces can be found
in caves under
the ground.

With this book,
you will be able
to observe the
secret world of
caves as if you
are really there.

As you explore the pages
of this book, a simple
paper flashlight will
reveal the world
inside the
earth.

Remove the paper flashlight from
the back of the book.

Move the flashlight between the black pages
and the plastic pages to discover hidden images.

Water flowing under the ground
dissolves rock, slowly creating a cave.
It takes thousands of years
for a cave to form.

soda straws

helectites

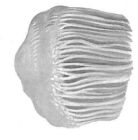

a jellyfish

drapery

Certain caves look like underground cathedrals. Water, falling drop by drop, leaves mineral deposits behind. As the mineral deposits build up, many strangely shaped sculptures appear.

Stalactites hang from the top of a cave, and stalagmites climb up from the cave floor. Sometimes the two meet to form a column.

a pile of plates

To descend into a cave, scale underground cliffs, and slide into narrow passageways, cave explorers—called cavers or spelunkers—need to have special equipment, and they must follow safety rules.

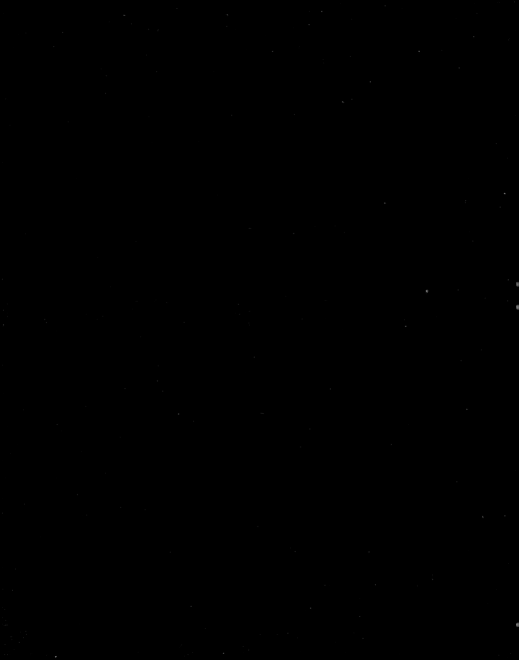

Some animals seek shelter in caves when they need to rest or bear their young. Other animals spend their entire lives in the depths of a cave. Because they live in darkness, most of these animals are blind and have colorless skin.

To get around in a cave, cavers sometimes need to cross a lake in an inflatable boat, then put on an air tank and go under water until they can climb back up.

In the shelter of a coral reef, where the sun's rays barely reach, divers discover caves and tunnels created by the movement of the water.

The Lascaux (lass-KOH) cave in France was discovered in 1940 by four boys who were looking for their dog. On the walls and ceiling of the cave, prehistoric humans had painted horses, bulls, and other animals.

Early humans worked by lamplight. Their lamps were made of sandstone and used animal fat for fuel. Painting was done with a hollow bone. Red or black paint was created with powders made from natural materials.

In the coldest parts of the world are ice caves. When the weather warms up, the snow in these caves melts and forms rivers. In the spaces created by these rivers, cavers and scientists can study ice that is hundreds of years old.

Anjou, France

Cappadoce, Turkey

Since prehistoric times, humans have found protection in natural gaps between rocks. Cave dwellers made their homes in these spaces. Whether they are used as homes or places to explore, caves are exciting places to visit.

In Colorado, visitors to Mesa Verde National Park can see cliff dwellings built by Pueblo people between A.D. 600 and A.D. 1300.

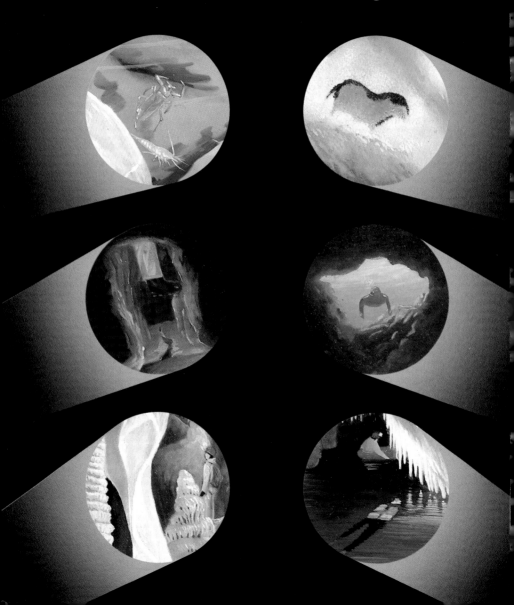

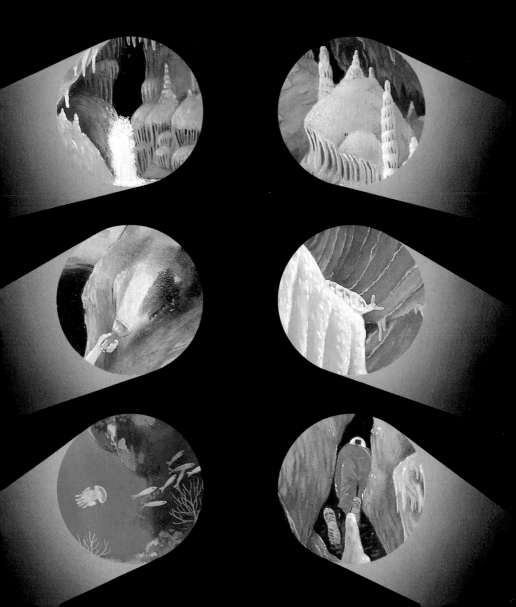

First Discovery Books:

**Airplanes
and Flying Machines
All About Time
Bees
Birds
Boats
Butterflies
The Camera
Cars and Trucks
and Other Vehicles
Castles
Cats
Colors
Construction
Dinosaurs
Dogs
The Earth and Sky
The Egg
Endangered Animals
Farm Animals
Fire Fighting
Fish**

**Flowers
Frogs
Fruit
Horses
Houses
The Human Body
The Ladybug and
Other Insects
Light
Monkeys and Apes
Musical Instruments
Native Americans
Night Creatures
Penguins
Pyramids
The Rain Forest
The River
The Seashore
Sports
Tools
Trains
The Tree
Turtles and Snails
Under the Ground**

**Universe
Vegetables in the
Garden
Water
Weather
Whales**

First Discovery
Atlas

**Atlas of Animals
Atlas of Countries
Atlas of the Earth
Atlas of Islands
Atlas of People
Atlas of Plants**

First Discovery
Hidden World

**Caves
Egyptian Tomb
Human Body
Under the Ground
Under the Sea**

Library of Congress Cataloging-in-Publication Data available.

Originally published in France in 1998 under the title *J'Observe: les grottes* by Editions Gallimard Jeunesse.

No part of this publication may be reproduced, or stored in a retrieval system, or transmitted in any form or by any means, electronic, mechanical, photocopying, recording, or otherwise, without written permission of the publisher. For information regarding permission, write to Scholastic Inc., Attention: Permissions Department, 555 Broadway, New York, NY 10012.

ISBN 0-439-10680-X

Copyright © 1998 by Editions Gallimard Jeunesse.
This edition English translation by Mary Varilla Jones. Copyright © 2000 by Scholastic Inc.
This edition American text by Mary Varilla Jones. Copyright © 2000 by Scholastic Inc.
This edition Expert Reader: National Speleological Society, Inc., Huntsville, AL

All rights reserved. First published in the U.S.A. in 2000 by Scholastic Inc. by arrangement with Editions Gallimard Jeunesse, 5 rue Sébastien-Bottin, F-75007, Paris, France.
SCHOLASTIC and A FIRST DISCOVERY BOOK and associated logos are trademarks and/or registered trademarks of Scholastic Inc.

10 9 8 7 6 5 4 3 2 1   00 01 02 03 04

Printed in Italy by Editoriale Lloyd

First Scholastic printing, March 2000